Fitting the Sixth Finger

Fitting the Sixth Finger

Poems inspired by the paintings of Marc Chagall

by
Gina Ferrara

Kelsay Books

Cover art: Marc Chagall

ISBN 13: 978-1-945752-54-4

Kelsay Books
Aldrich Press
www.kelsaybooks.com

For Jonathan

Acknowledgments

Grateful acknowledgment is made to the editors of the following journals and publications for publishing these poems:

The Maple Leaf Rag Volume V: "Almost"
Cafe Luna Review: "Hemorrage"
Mockingheart Review: "The Moon Painter"
Cultural Vistas: "One Village Defined"

"Ethereal Avalanche", "Explained in Color", "Fitting the Sixth Finger", "From Dirt", "Indigo Stirrings", "Over the Village", and "Yesterday's Explanation", first appeared in *Ethereal Avalanche,* published by Trembling Pillow Press, 2009.

Sincere thanks and gratitude to friends and colleagues who kindly offered encouragement and support: Missy Abbott, Ralph Adamo, Nordette Adams, Stacey Balkun, Jack Bedell, Steve Beisner, Marilyn Bohren, Darrell Bourque, Brian Boyles, Dave Brinks, Megan Burns, Chris Champagne, Thaddeus Conti, Peter Cooley, Emily Cosper, Jim Davis, David DeGeorge, Michael Fedor, Dennis Formento, Kathleen Gallante, Elizabeth Garcia, John Gery, Patty Glaser, Lee Grue, Kelly Harris, Nancy Harris, Ava Leavell Haymon, Carolyn Hembree, Linda and Jackson Hill, Moose Jackson, Sara Jacobelli, Sandra Johnson, Julie Kane, Pat Kaschalk, Herbert Kearney, Danny Kerwick, Jonathan Kline, Katheryn Krotzer Laborde, Susan Larson, Melanie Leavitt, Tom Lowenberg, Clare Martin, Monica Mankin, Laura Mattingly, Carol McCarthy, Judy Mixon, Benjamin Morris, Sean Munro, Geoff Munsterman, Biljana Obradovic, Izzie Oneric, Melinda Palacio, Valentine Pierce, Deborah Reed, Miranda Restovic, Jimmy Ross, David Rowe, Dodd Schweinfurth, Kari Shisler, Penny Speaker, John Travis, Jerry Ward, Laura Weeks, Laurie Williams, Andy Young, Ari Zeigler

Contents

III. Imaged

IV. Beheld

About the Author

I. Observed

A Study in Red

The moon's own corona

shines with a pink exclusivity

at apex in the curving sky

and full above the village in ascent

with russet rooftops, this place of nascence,

itself, my teacher in all things—

the baker, the bustle,

the farmer, the blacksmith's

sparks, the sommelier

who picks and dries his leaves

for what is steeped

and lingers at the cup's bottom.

I am bathed in red

with knowledge

and curled like a comma,

a much needed pause

before ending.

After the First Flood

That spectrum, settling, appears after hallelujahs
and heartbreak, the start and finish
of intangible hues progressing then retreating,
if only for a moment.

A drab, sleepy life stirs
by what is untouched overhead,
what isn't lost, but will be—a slipping moment
more ethereal than imagination.

How can light be an apparition,
a bridge uncrossed, one promise
that lacks stones, steps, or solidity—
to stand beneath, to give unspoken reason
for a lasting gaze?

An Ethereal Avalanche

You are a Parisian bridge
stretched flat across the river
wearing a coat woven from twilight.
A dexterous muse waits to play the violin.
You sleep with a palette where paint
forms its own exquisite solar system,
colored drops revolve like planets
around your invisible sun
until you wake on this night and paint us
over the moon's surface.
An ethereal avalanche
some will only recognize as moonlight
shines on steeples and hills.
It is our bliss.
You and I give this city light.
Those bleeding hearts you impetuously picked
graze my veil as dabs from a dream
before falling slowly into the river.

Flipped

My feet lost their desire making steps.
I stand on my head in the dark
with cheeks slightly pink
from blood steadily rushing.
My delighted soles are in the air
and face a full moon.
I could remove your hat,
hook its brim
with a flick of my heel.
This only presents a problem
when we dance.
The neighbor stares through the lower window pane.
He suspects you have turned me upside down.

Becoming Palpable

Bliss goes aerial, grows palpable
over a red house and wooden fence
in the afternoons after the revolution—

the decision you make to take me
in flight to leave the sinewy roots
and the myriad of their complexities.

Your lips still bear ripened wonder,
skin and pulp, the purpose of your first kiss—
fullness needs one response,
to sate what isn't stated.

Before Occupying Center Ring

Pliable as lemon taffy and whims,
I contort, ecstatic on a horse's back
limber on one foot
I raise my leg, in arabesque,
stretch it toward the fullest moon
like my last exaggeration.

Before the swell, the calliope's call,
I study the acrobat unbound
who swings over the bar—
the sinewy back, the taut torso
moves in clockwise and counterclockwise hours
corner to corner jacquard trapezoids of touching colors
above an audible sea of sudden gasps.

While the Sky Convalesces

The sky convalesces.
Here, there are no upside down
women or headless men.
I'm done with self portraits
and knives stuck in wood.
Conversations are better left
to the imagination than photographed.
The ground is colored as confetti
or a heap of taffeta the morning after.
The audacious earth appears yellow
and rises like a song.
Soon the birds and rooster will arrive.
Shellfish remain shelled in the purple river.
Nothing amphibious swims
near my house, slightly askew with blue
logs swaying to their own imagined rhythm.

Before the Poem Took Form

I never wrote of candy luminous skies,
entendres of violets and greens,
the edible things adrift spun from air

though I saw the pink clouds,
their sweet sashays and segues
solidity nearly reached—

how they tinged the background exactly
in a shade of fluster or mild embarrassment,
a silent but delicate rush of blood beneath the skin.

One evening, minutes before dusk encroached,
I reclined in a grazing field,
my sweat touching soft blades.

The mare and newly fleeced ewe
chewed the earth, the verdant continuation
before the poem took form.

Between Blunt Blade and Handle

It began in pencil.
The point defining as my mania grew
sleepless in the heat—
no time to erase
rapid strokes on paper,
the wound sprawled
a dripping sun
above the wheat field,
a virgin bull's eye
center intact as a perfect red pupil.
I saw in a field afire
the distance between
blunt blade and handle,
a saffron sky framed
by the scythe
you once held,
blade glinting with the sheen of a wish

Blurriness and Belief

Shield your eyes.
Pack your sack.
Fling burlap over your shoulder.
Flames rise from paper houses,
or wind topples them.
Fire destroys those made of stone.
Let the lions beneath David's star
maim and paw.
Does the ocean ever quell what's started?
Notes remain unfinished
near the overturned chair.
Only three rungs,
your past, present, and future,
left to climb on the ladder.
The book, unbound, no longer writes itself,
stanzas turn to ether.
Blurriness, like belief,
comes and goes.
The path divides us like a crucifixion.
Cram your thoughts between two black lines.
That fringe on the shroud grazes the knees
and hangs flammable.
Soon it will ignite.

Bolder than Celadon

Unable to strike the right hour,
the clock keeps a silent kind of time,
every hour its own duration
for arriving and leaving,
an imposing tower
with a face for each direction
ready to greet the wind.
In that first hour after noon,
you arrive exclamatory
on a jade green horse,
a single stance and statement
bolder than celadon
blowing your trumpet
as I write another page,
different than yesterday's finish.

Where Thawing Begins

I am the tactile comet
never hurting your hand
as it seeks my red orange tail
shooting silk and tulle,
a tangible dichotomy, meant
to pass through your fingers
on this cold night.

The rooster beside me, made of ice, turns—
his glistening plumes, a spectacle of shavings
and crystals soon descend
on pitched roofs.
The iridescent lovers kiss
close to the cusp of purple
where thawing always begins.

Fitting the Sixth Finger

The wall peels back, as all bandages do,
in a yellow room. Askance, askew,
the table has the flaw of a nose.
Tenses of time are held in our cups.
My chin points toward heaven, a flame forms
my right hand. I will write later.
The silver carafe answers questions
of who and why our dog understands.
Your extra finger is neither a curse nor blessing.
I will sew your glove and give you one more ring.
Speak to me, my love, though the hemorrhaging moon
has turned the sky red over rooftops.
Remember this morning when news began
folded at your feet?

II. Discernible

Over the Village

When plum blossoms part slower than a kiss,
the iridescence is caught for a moment
between layers of wool and words.
I'll give you memories of a green hat
glinting with bugle beads and painted buttons.
Your plume brushes my skin.
Our handful of pearls needs string tonight
and you will tie the knots.
We float near the silent violin.
The white light emanates
as a beautiful oracle above the apexes of trees.
How many times can we see the moon together?

Charlie Chaplin in Portrait

My mother's voice fell off the cliff
never to be retrieved when I took the spotlight

and sang with a cracking voice
a golden yolk emerging from fragility

to complete what she started
evolving to stand before the camera

as a soft shoed vagabond
my suit dusted in factory soot,

and my gait a balancing act
of shifting scales as I shuffled

a parrot's walk holding my props:
the onyx walking stick,

the handle carved in cursive
and my solitary wing

that never enabled me to fly
or to reach a point of apogee.

My shoes wouldn't keep pace.
It was nothing to stand on my hands

to press my fingers to the floorboards
to walk away without soliloquizing.

Contemplating the Red Road

To sit like a stone first chiseled by Rodin
before taking expression—
the pairings never appear.
One dove roosts on the roof,
a solitary cow grazes,
a lone fiddle is silent and idle.
I contemplate the permanence
of India ink, the solid black
pigment, the daily compressions
and my restless hand seeking
to sketch what has yet to appear.
How is it that I am still alive
surviving those childhood
crucifixions on slack crosses
where the red road was swept
of everything but its distance?

Without Theory

For some it is a day of sabbath,
a day of worship, a day of fresh loaves
and sweet cream to spread.
On this day, I have no extra fingers
to glove or groom, to dip in my palette,
to color the sky mauve,
or to dabble with the dotted
light of constellations.
The sprig of flowers falls
from your hair an ornamental cascade
left unbraided, the days of distance
are milk coated and without pallor.
Together I paint us my own
holy trinity of man, woman,
and moon, the place of
eminence synonymous
with risen.

Creation

Abandoning the loom and a myriad of threads
in sapphire, spun saffron and aubergine,
my hands sought copper plates,
shiny aluminum,
the proverbial weight
of stone, to etch meaning,
to retain and repel ink absent of rhetoric,
engraving all my joys and sorrows
surrounded by rose petals and prolific wheat,
prophets, lovers, fiddlers…a large iridescent fish
without a school in the bay of wingless angels.
The flutist called up the sun
an improvised genesis in short, effortless breaths.

The Divine Eruption

In my gray world
of charcoal, granite, and mortar
the pallor of mediocrity pervades
where ugly things mesh with beauty
like wrong and right,
like individuality and industry.

I look over my shoulder
expecting to see my past,
some hapless crucifixion
punctuated by wood and nails,
a hammer driven into the outstretched arm,
the bent feet of supplication.

From the unnamed volcano
the archangel emerges
a divine eruption
less forceful than soot and ash
inspiration spewing
wayward locks and impressively winged
ready to annunciate
without saying a word,
until, I too, believe
in the authenticity of blue.

Explained in Color

Look inside these large, stained glass shards.
Hold them toward the sun
or turn the kaleidoscope clockwise
and we will appear.
What's seen as collage I write
in fragments, a blue wedding day
beneath the umbrella, a baldachin,
when I fished for the ring
to place on your hand,
my pocket a tepid pond—
the Eiffel Tower rose red
beneath a feverish sky,
the city infected with hatred, and occupation
trains arriving and departing with
loathsome punctuality— a green room
safety finally found in a patina,
the table almost an apparition,
the simplicity of flowers revolving
above the large vase,
anything but a still life—
and in orange, a bright omega,
the flare seen in a sky, a comet's tail
where the rooster walked away
from the painted you
and me on the easel
only color could explain.

The Golden Sky

There's cause for a golden sky.
I'm inspired by honey's
perfect viscosity
that holds my spoon upright.
This color will never dissolve
nor will the raised scar
from an old wound.
Sweetness lingers and is best remembered
as your favorite couplet.
We live and love in a double portrait.
Unfold your eloquent fan
in shades of magenta with its silken
filament stitches, steady as laughter.
A jester cloud passes.
This filled goblet at noon
is higher than any sun.
I'll cover only one of your eyes.
You'll need the other to search
the bottom of an emerald sea.

The Village Mother

Is the village mother an ideal,

an enigma, a white apparition?

You have seen her, recognized

her omniscience.

Without flesh or verbs she hovers

sinewy in her furlongs

like some sort of silent witness

above the ghettos and guillotines

where humanity deserts itself

in those times of genocide.

From Any Defined Spot

In pink, gray, green,
and sandstorm,
some would say it's cardinal,
obvious as all four directions
how I've depicted us—
my face obscured only by yours
touching lip to lip,
the splendid leaves of Eden,
in the dream,
a fluid embrace,
timeless profiles
on canvas and board.
My eye unintentionally obscured,
the vision eclipsed
by the mere frill and ruffle
of sheer lace.

When Rhymes Run Out of Reason

A merlot ring rimmed
the decanter's bottom.
We ran out of rhymes then reasons.
Two golden apples left on the plate
were perfect subjects of a still life.

Your black suit remained unstained.
The linen got looser.
We had our fill of grapes,
goat cheese and celery stalks.

My silk kimono
slid into an orange heap on the grass
in this city where rooftops
and the promenade are darker
than evergreen.

None of the azure leaves fell.
I spun around twice
holding your hand
as I levitated higher
than a pink kite
above the faint rotunda.

From Dirt

Why should we gather the stars?
Answers arrive from dirt.
Brown-eyed Susans and daisies
rise from the pitcher.
Sent from the sun,
the essence of yes is never
more yellow than today.
How long will it last?
Known for brevity
we dance in a mist
more about light than
textured cumulus
mysteriously adrift.
The cardinal needs no nest
and loses its want for branches,
here with us,
where the basket of fruit
picked ripe sits certain
on gingham.

Half Past Three

Starting, then restarting,
a crumpled page
an abandoned metaphor
when I've spread
the last soft pat of butter,
a dark corona
rims the white cup.
The inspiration comes
with the momentum of a squall
once seen on the beach—
a deluge in an instant
cloudbursts, ideas, drastic pelts
cold bullets dropping,
oranges and wildflowers
scatter a drum in my head
moving counterclockwise
lost time with slant rhymes,
stray cats and imperfect meters.

The verse I've written
stays freer than any wind.

III. Imaged

Held in an Hour

The same hour holds what has passed
and what has yet to come.
We will not fall into the red abyss
part of our vows never said at the altar
in the temple of memory.

The neophyte lights the candle,
chars the wick and scoops the wax.
A perfect circle is another year passing.

Those chips of color surround us—
ever changing visual symphonies,
each a gem tone that hums
between citrine and ruby.

The first person omniscient
depicts the village, houses
without doors, recessed rotundas,
the olive tree's crooked trunk,
and dreams of the decade—
the recurring one of the milkmaid:
her pail in hand, she pulls the udder
and teat of a cow without marks
whiter than the milk it offers.

Hemorrhage

By needle, nail, or blade,

blood arrives as one

bubbling droplet, the red

unabashed bead when the skin breaks;

but what about the brush

quicksilver with its dipped bristles

stroking the taut white expanse

until that hemorrhage of blue,

the dark rush of it

forms last night's Parisian sky?

Unleashed Fire in the Snow

Green smoke crosses oceans.
The baby touches its eye and sees
green smoke in the snow,
has no memory of the verdant.
I notice the size of my hands.
What? What can I do?
I didn't set it though I piled the sticks.
Everything burns green, even
the town, a wound on the hill
burns, growing greener and gangrenous.
I can barely see the little white dog.
It blends in the snow and
leaves no paw prints,
like a four-legged phantom
without a collar or tag.
The dog turns to look,
and walks unleashed
away from this fire in the snow.

Indigo Stirring and Strings

Doves, bluebirds and memorized couplets
come from my fiddle.
They cannot nest.
All my life I dodged syllables and dictionaries
knowing that words break and retain meaning.
I play notes with both hands
though the one seen glows white.
I've no fingers to spare.
The bouquet with its filament blossoms
spills in moonlight.
I sit in the four-cornered world
above your silent village
where there are no trees.
Who can control a cowlick,
the way I live?
The indigo grows restless.
I see it stirring.
Soon, it will wake you as a bow
virtuosity recognized, rubbed
against strings.

Lamentations of a Lesser Hand

The left hand can seldom stay still
after it opens jars
and sets the fireflies free.
They ignite the woods in single syllables,
diphthongs and ampersands.
Each finger stretches
and seeks the dark dirt of continents
breaking clumps of earth
for the tossed and migratory seed.
A fiddle and bow rest against a tree.
Virtuosity never stares at its own reflection.
It blooms for more than a season
The first note played pierces the placid
as that nascent moment never to be repeated.

Mere Metres from Avignon

In my still life, two vases,
one onyx, the other pewter,
never touched though they shared
fragrant bouquets, what came
from seed or bulb.

The pink sky was a deceptive sky
nearly flesh toned that far south
without a sun, maybe a hint
of blood beneath its surface—
the armistice signed in cursive
protected that point of apex
the place of unwritten poems,
the picturesque village
of clean streets and shutters agape
while the war with its occupations
and holocaust raged.

News never came to the garden
on those days when the lavender
rambled over the arch and trellis.

In their boxes, the geraniums remained red.

My Real Home

If it weren't for the wind, some pages never would
turn in an open book. We have the perfect end
on a day of beginnings. The three-horned goat
emerges from the mist. Darker than a sapphire,
the Eiffel Tower without filigree rises lighter
than the night sky. Napoleon's tomb remains gold
as the ring I placed earlier on your finger,
one of six you have on your hand.
A cello levitates and fills the ether
with vibratory tones. Mandolin strings are heard
near the Seine. I left scrolled calla lilies on the altar
and hold the blue borrowed fan next to frothing lace.
Do not weep for the russet earth.
We left the dream to live it.

In the Span of Your Name

It seemed perfect
how the first and last
began the same
harboring a certain alliteration
and syllabic count like feet ascending
eight stone steps,
sounding purely casual and almost happenstance
until appearing in slants and cursive loops
resembling small nooses.
I said nothing about
the authenticity of origin
and bloodlines that couldn't be changed—
the hard consonants of it and the letters that stood
silent as stalactites
in the span of your name.

One Slack Hour

It was not Sunday,
but soft and dusky
a worn blue yesterday,
a durable sky,
blue chambray
becoming undone.

My eyes affixed
on your throat
to the single rivulet
the delicacy of sweat
and how it traveled
seen to unseen
its own triumphant tributary.

I hoarded words meant to describe
the way you looked like one slack hour,
an abundant heap of minutes
able to bloom like fire
with or without air.

Unparted

Aubades will not be written
today, a slow ascent
that brings the beast we share
nearly yellow neon red blooded
one mammalian cloud with hooved feet
that never grazes the fields.

Without the burden of wings
the quotidian arrives, two eggs,
uncracked as a couplet.

A full branch detaches,
one shared affirmation,
when the cock crows
once and only once:
its tail and plumage spread
splendid origins and red dawns.

Paying Visual Homage

To paint a mood,

an innate feeling, a sudden

flash of intuition rather than a time

marked by war or inventions

means removing the black glove,

the solitary one worn during the heist.

No faces will stand out

in the deep scope of this blue,

bluer than the delphiniums

or hyacinths,

more tranquil than sorrowful.

One temple is any temple.

The houses of this moment

are melodious as a nocturne

rising and falling

along my road that celebrates

the avoidance of anything rendered

linear.

Rapidity

I grow weary of your right angle
formations, the upright, outstretched aspects
of your personality and how they hold
the house on the brink of an avalanche
stucco and lumber cascading
only to devastate the low valley,
the unsuspecting village.

Look in the mirror
for a righteous reflection
of watercolor and ink, marks on gouache
as you carry the abode on your back,
the borrowed ideas swirling beneath rafters.

Smoke wafts, curls a question
in willowy ascent,
the way you mimic quick cadences,
trendy causes and my brush strokes
wanting break bark and wood,
before taking flight.

Procession in Vitebsk

Sleeping in that inner sanctum—
that place of encouragement
inside the cortex
where words formed,
I awoke to the smell of caught herrings
being gutted and scaled,
followed by a wedding procession,
the indispensable fiddle annunciating,
filling stony crevices
and cracks between the living and the dead
the somber streets—
their drab stretches of distance
uplifted by the sight of netting,
a cloud of nuptial tulle
coming from the hill.

IV. Beheld

Almost

your smile, an enigma,
no longer endless, given
like some private corridor of potential
a place between once upon a time
and happily ever after
my frequent return
waiting for the water
you brought without spilling a drop—
the cubes of ice, six unmelting
sides, sharp edges without shards
floating in self blown glass
what you carried, the well's riches
emptied from a carafe
to quench my thirst on an August day
when that fragmented rainbow
appeared without its arc,
a pale spectrum, almost
anemic and good enough
for half a wish.

Tangled in Twine

Unlike explanations, cubes have six sides.
I see only five.
Don't call me a drunkard.
The wine is postured for pouring.
The red Siamese birds search for crumbs
in a footed bowl.
The frenzied sand fly swarm left.
No one joins me for dinner.
My severed head distracts them
with its ability to drift
over harbors and empty fields
away from my vertebrae.
It seeks only the vineyard.
I hold the knife, blade down ready
to gut my father's blue fish.
I, too, was caught in his nets.

Spanning the Spectrum

Struggling to say ascent and descent
in a language that wasn't my mother's,
I see the steeples and rotundas.
Bread rises in the oven.
One hour arrives with feather and wing.
I've brought myself here again
beneath the changing blue
a saturated sky spanning the spectrum
of a dream realized
by walking the hills and dusty paths,
the idle fiddle beneath the tree.
After opening my eyes,
the yellow galoshes
with straps and buckles
weren't worn for those ninety-nine rainless days,
yet here I am reciting fragmented prayers,
the months and birthstones
without stopping at rubies in July.

The Artist Paints His Brother

This act of convalescing,
a footed bowl of tepid broth
that took on clouds in the afternoon —
one personal aftermath remained unwritten
by the open window in abrupt syllables
of necessary answers…pecans fell prematurely
pummeling the roof pitched like a pair of prayerful hands
while David played the mandolin
after untangling the strings
stretching their length to potential longitudes—
crossing those never visited lands.
His jacket, frayed, without patches,
hung green as the last casaba that ripened.

The Endless Vocabulary

Arrayed with colorful little sparks
the lavender lantana erupted
out of the ground, a tangle
of thin branch and vine,
another page torn without perforation
the cosmos brighter
than any kumquat
dropped seeds
to replant and proliferate
the endless vocabulary
of creation, papaya,
pear, pomegranate,
our catalog of pulp.
It was only a matter of time,
the knowledge, the awareness
loomed larger than the slant
rhyme of saffron and bovine
before we shared
the perfect peach.

One Jester's Dilemma

The jester wears statements of generosity
billowy green sleeves flouncing
ruffles against wrists
and six strings of strength as a shield.
With his torn pages from an unbound book,
he is not shallow, humming in low vibratory tones.

What to juggle? The list continues
with the artichoke and orange:
those surface causes and tired ideologies
as the circle of one-eyed onlookers
anticipate the arc, this half of the world
dreaming of epics and points and wide angles.

The Moon Painter

Without gravity I paint the moon,

how the strokes swirl like whispers

in preferred shades and hushed tones,

lavender emerges always

in the backdrop of my dreams

when I am somnambulatory

the knife spreads the subdued

beams and unbroken coronas—

my footsteps fade like laughter

swift then elliptic,

I stifle those late night yawns

and prismatic searches—

trails of syllables converge.

The curtains printed with words

billow until they become voluminous

with meaning.

The Bèrgere

Heisted from Versailles
yesterday, a seat of shared
pink peony bliss, parenthetically
open arms and tufted velveteen.

Our room has this
and only this, one solitary chair
absent of tables, added names and acrobats,
no mirrors or trumeaus
or upturned hook for the umbrella.

Seventeen syllables
could only partially describe
the afternoon, an unpainted landscape,
shadows appearing like virtuosity
from the flustered flock,
the collective ripening of rinds and skin
beneath the open window.

The Roof Grows Red

A bow moves in the space
between narrow longitudes
and what's eternally parallel.
With his only follower,
the fiddler has one eye open
and the other closed to the world's
apparitions and horizons.
He gets by with his half vision,
his unfinished sentences,
and not knowing who won the war,
or which son was born.

The Ungrounded Hour

Gold appears,
even with one wing
tufted in deep blue down,
a blue, more authentic than ink.
I am airborne, an hour ungrounded,
free of measure not meant for precision
or punctuality
I levitate hovering above a milky village
windows, naked, lanterns dimmed
on a moonless night when lovers kiss—
a couplet of arrival or departure
untouched by the pendulum.

As If Turned Upside Down

Unable to live with dark spots
and the stylized,
my eyes had their revolution—
the flowers bloomed short of shadows
unable to rise to full stature
grazing the ankles rather than shoulders.

The cosmos opened and dropped seeds
the size of splinters
for red horses and father-son acrobats to appear,
to tumble and stretch towards the sun,
to lay out their dirty carpet
with unbridled edges,
to perform like the greatest
source of poetry of all time.

This gift of honest hues and dappled light
was what I dreamed—
the assumption of ten crows black arches
flying over grain days before harvest
and a hurled moon stopping
over a second birthplace
between pinnacles of leafless trees.

The Unnamed Wind

You are the fifth direction,
the repeatedly espoused
in this life and past ones,
the unnamed wind,
the center's circle,
the identified self, nameless,
a truth blowing across the village
with smokestacks standing
as unhinged trilogies, the unspoken
direction that never appears
upright on a map or compass,
recognized by the avian alphabet,
an entry between gusts,
ghazals, gales, gazelles,
exhilarating exhales,
a choreography of possibilities
beyond the temple's top.

Yesterday's Explanation

Immortalized on cardboard
our images are rendered in oil
now that you've put away the matches
and the nagging cough left.
The sky has no sun.
Nothing will burn.
Air fills the lungs white as light.
We see the oxygen
above a row of brown bungalows.
The village inhales, turns on its side
restful as a dog.
I could be a planet floating pinkly.
No, I'm a lotus in a pond,
a folded offering, yesterday's explanation.
Who severed us in half, my love,
I ask, moving closer to your lips.
Was the blade buried?
Speak only after we kiss.

About the Author

Gina Ferrara lives in New Orleans and has several collections of poems that include *The Size of Sparrows* (Finishing Line Press 2006) *Ethereal Avalanche* (Trembling Pillow Press 2009) *Amber Porch Light* (CW Books 2013) and *Carville: Amid Moss and Resurrection Fern* (FLP 2014). She teaches English and creative writing at Delgado Community College and is a guest artist at the Low Residency MFA Program at the University of New Orleans. Her poetry has appeared in *Callaloo, anderbo, Valley Voices* and others. She has received grants from the Louisiana Division of the Arts and The Elizabeth George Foundation. Since 2007 she has been curating The Poetry Buffet, a monthly reading series presented by the New Orleans Public Library.